I0182566

WAITING FOR THE MOON

WAITING FOR THE MOON

New Poems

Janice Kochanski

FCP

Full Court Press
Englewood Cliffs, New Jersey

First Edition

Copyright © 2015 by Janice Kochanski

Published in the United States of America
by Full Court Press, 601 Palisade Avenue,
Englewood Cliffs, NJ 07632
fullcourtpressnj.com

ISBN 978-1-938812-74-3

*Book design by Barry Sheinkopf for Bookshapers.Com
(www.bookshapers.com)*

Cover art, "Hudson River, 2015," by Barry Sheinkopf

Colophon by Liz Sedlack

TO MY FATHER
who taught me to strive

AND TO ROY LUCIANNA
*who encouraged me
unfailingly*

TABLE OF CONTENTS

ACTING CLASS

Did you know I've been acting
for years
smiling and laughing politely
at your not-too-funny jokes
sitting through another
boring dinner
looking sadly disappointed
when I expect, yet don't,
excuses for your lateness.

Shall I tell my acting coach
of these and of my other
star performances?
I think
I'd rather sit here quietly,
making believe
I'm not nervous.

A MOTHER'S PAIN

I never knew
a mother's pain
could be so deep
Disability
and death
and disappointment
are all things
that we don't think of
when we're having children
ripping our hearts
into shreds

CATS WITH
STRANGE MEOWS

Cats with strange meows
dogs barking in whimpers
people talking
So much noise

Where is the quiet
I so need
but try to get away from?

CELL PHONE

Pick up the damn phone
if you can
ringing in your pocket
scaring the contents
of your pocketbook

Yet they don't
so busy are they

Just text me
they say

No
it's a voice
I want to hear
not typed-out words.

CLOTHES
IN THE WINDOWPANES

I like to dry
my clothes in the window,
see them dancing in the wind,
clean and crisp
and calling to me,
When can you wear us again?

DON'T COUNT

Don't count on me
My life changes
minute to minute
A call and I am gone
out the door
Dinner and fun
Disappointment
for those who try to plan
Don't count on me.

ENTANGLEMENT

Entangled like a fly in a web
I am stuck
strands of silk reaching
searching for a hold

Escaping I jump
running fast as a gazelle
coming back to find
it was only a dream of freedom
the silken web
too strong for me

INJURED EAGLE

You, eagle, hit by a car,
with your broken wing,
and I with my broken spirit,
are one--
unable to fly again
but grounded
by the earth
to see close up
the depths
in every grain of sand.

MARINATED CHICKEN

I soak you in
like chicken
marinating
in oil and lemon juice

Each word
each gesture
move
seeps into me
spicing up my skin.

OBJECTS

Each little object
such a beauty:
cute little green calculator
waiting to add or subtract;
deep red drinking glasses
standing next to each other,
hoping for someone's lips
to graze them.
"De-clutter. Get rid of things,"
they say, but what if
the new owners
don't see their beauty?

GLOVES IN THE SNOW

A random black glove
crushed and dirty
lies in the snow.
Little mitten so pink,
where are you?
They jump out of your
pockets
to try to be on their own.
You are not, lost glove.
I see you sorry now
to have tried to leave.

REACTION

Sadly I declare
it's me
not them
those I have
been angry at
and blamed
have criticized
and thought about
how unfairly I was treated
I was too quick
to feel the stab
of their pushpins

SEARCHING

Searching clothing racks,
furniture stores, movie theatres:
Entertain me,
world.
Give me something brand new.
Doesn't matter how much I pay--
happiness on a credit card,
disappointment
as soon as I get home.

SHED TO COLOR

The sidewalk
came to life
today
in fact
was covered
in a red and orange-yellow
blanket
slippery and wet

Such a healthiness
of leaves
shed to color
on our dirty walkway.

SINGING BOWL

The sound reverberates
inside my soul

It tingles up my spine
centering my balance
the ringing going on and on
right through my ears
into my throat
connecting me to everything.

SLY FOX

Entice me with manipulation
subtle with nicety.
Falling into the trap
I settle in
expecting to notice
your sly tricks.
I don't. You're too good
at this game:
fooled again.

SURRENDER

Surrender
is a funny friend

Once you let it go
you get much more
than you were
holding onto.

TALK

Nagging words
in my head
won't leave,
telling me
the old
stories and lies.
Truth hangs up
in the clouds,
never raining down--
dries up before
it hits my mind.

THE RIGHTEOUS

So much emphasis on being right.
Who cares, maybe I'm wrong,
And if you are right
Who cares?
Do you get a medal for that?
Each of us has our own ideas.
Let's stop being right and arguing.
Husbands and wives,
You are all right.

LOOKING FOR GOD

I am always looking for God
up in the sky in my heart
walking in the street

There he was
a book
lost
dirty from bible class
uniting us.

TUG OF WAR

I set the boundaries up
you push them back

I silently beseech
you benefit

I ignore you
but you call me back

You're testing me
but I'm not playing

WARM SOCKS

Soaking wet
sneakers
socks drenched
feet frozen like
blocks of ice
warm socks
dry cotton
slip onto
my frozen feet

WATERFALL

Grief washed over me
like a waterfall
strong and soaking
shrinking my joy
kerchiefed in black
cloaked in sorrow
gripping my soul

WHERE, WHEN, AND WHO

Dreaming where
knowing when
remembering who
keeps me busy
all day long.

WINTER WOES

O winter, you are wicked
and clean but harsh.
Shades drawn to stop breezes,
darkness envelopes me;
spring hints: daffodils,
and warmth, and renewal.

YOU AND I ARE ONE

You and I are one
Hating your neediness
which is mine too
refusing your requests
knowing they're not
what you're asking for
but a piece of me
which is you
I cannot help you
find yourself

NO ONE IS HERE

"No one is here to answer your call.
Please leave a message."
They all do,
Telling me things they wouldn't
If I'd answered.
If I say, "Hello?"
They're disappointed.
"Oh, I thought the machine'd answer!"
I've figured it out--
They want to talk to themselves.

SUNDOG

Sundog in the cold
October morning sky
brightening white clouds
with color a reminder
of light in the darkness
of our soul.

PUPPIES FROLIC

Puppies frolic
kittens meow
living in cages
sold for pets
to families
who can't
keep up already

They bring them home
complain about the mess
The puppies grow up into dogs
kittens into cats
left alone
wondering
why this family
took them

4 A.M.

4 a.m.
dogs barking loudly
neighbors awakening
eviction soon

Shut up
please
Quiet down
What do you want?
Are there demons
and goblins flying
around--
or maybe the silence
needs your screeching?

FLOWERS OF THOUGHT

Flowers of thought
spring forth
a petal at a time
connected to the stem
of an idea

Deeply down
the roots feed
memory

FLYING MONEY

It flew across
the driveway
that twenty-dollar bill--
I caught it
with my eye
but left it there
for those
who owned it
when they came
out later.

FRIENDS

To my friends,
waiting for me
to write a poem
about them,
shall I tell
about their lies,
misfortunes, or their
lack of caring?
Best we leave
them out of it.
Yes, of course, their patience,
kindness, love--
but aren't these prerequisites
for friendship?

OLD OAK

The tree men came
this morning
at seven a.m.
with their tools.

I heard
the chainsaw,
felt so sad.
The old oak
was only half alive
yet she and I
had shared so much
of wind and rain
sunlight and snow.

She's gone now,
where she stood
an open field
now bright with sunshine
and my memories
of her stale beauty.

SEVEN HAIKU

1.

Air rips in
like a sharp sword sinks in flesh.
So long the cold lasts

2.

People are sleeping
in stairwells. o winter, you,
wicked clean but harsh.

3.

Drawn shades stop breezes:
Darkness envelops me; spring
hints daffodil warmth.

4.

azure butterfly
surprising us all morning
flitting in the sun

5.
Kildeers running fast
The mom feigns broken wing to
confuse predators

6.
Fireflies sparking bright:
Dusk takes over; moon rises
over the river.

7.
Dark clouds are tinged green
And echo now with thunder:
Rain pounds the pavement.

LOST SOUL

Hard walls
of concrete
hold up
the building

She hurries frantically
into each
room,
searching
for her soul

which she lost
some time ago.

BLUE JAY

You told me once
you were a blue jay
in another life.
As I heard him screaming
I knew you were still okay.

Now you're gone
and I hear the blue jay
blue and white
symbolizing Heaven and Earth.

CERAMIC BOWLS

Ceramic bowls with cardinals
Empty I gave them
You love them
Good for soup or cereal

In return you handed me
plastic containers
filled with chili
What an exchange
empty ceramics
for plastic full of food

CHANGELING

Smiling, you see my face.
Words ignite a rage.
Flooding sobs engulf.
Daggers of resentment stab.
Doves,
emotional complexities,
surround me.

EXPECTATIONS

Promises that did not know the lies
Good intentions falling down

Disappointment settles in
Expectations start again

HOBO

He skipped across the railroad tracks
with a hat too big for his head—
dwarflike man or boy
smiling in his oversized shoes
with nowhere to go.

INVISIBLE CLOTHES

I'm trucking around
an invisible vest of shame and guilt
covered by a jacket of pride,
belly full of beer
held in by a belt of bravado.

Laughter escapes me
mixed with fear,
my shoes encasing socks
made up of layers of mistakes.

FENCE

The suburbs are filled
with couples
that hate each other
who resent the fence
invisible
yet so restrictive
like a necklace
too tight around their necks
hopes turned into a nightmare
of silently watching
TV every night
and eating snacks

dreaming of freedom

LOVE OF ALCOHOL

Noontime
liquor store

spellbound
with desire

salivating
in anticipation

of the drink
that is breaking up
his marriage

God can't help it
A power greater
than His will
has taken over

MEMENTOS OF YOU

I keep on saving
mementos of you

ties you wore
army pictures
when you were so strong

remembering the weakness
and fear you lived with
fighting for your country
and at the end
of your life

MISERY

You came
and sat with me
in my misery

unblinking
and steady
as a lighthouse
not judging
but knowing

It only takes
compassion
to melt the stain away

STORMS OF EMOTION

Rain and wind
pulverize me
soaking through my pants

I smile
used to storms
of emotion
confusion
and chaos

knowing this
won't last long
that the sun will come out soon
and all will be forgotten
till the next time comes

TEACH ME
HOW NOT TO BE

You show me
how inconsiderate
not to be

Thank you
for lessons
in Not

Simple words you speak
disgusting
with resentment
make me deplore
your hatred

I try to show you
patience
but you crumple it
up like
loose-leaf paper

Just thought

how lucky I am
to know you
and be me

THE FIREHOUSE CAT

Orange tabby with a blue collar
struts around like a fireman
in my driveway,
driving the dogs mad
crossing streets. The cars stop.
"Pick him up!" a woman shouts
out of a car window.
The kid does and gets scratched.
Three kids by the creek
try to steal him,
but he evades their grasp--
prowling around, saved by the firemen.

THINKING ABOUT
MY THINKING

Thinking about my thinking
makes me wonder,
Where have these thoughts
come from?
Am I brainwashed?
I stop thinking and think
some more.

WINTER NIGHT

The shovel scrapes the concrete
as the plow flies down the street

Dogs frolic
kids throw snowballs
at my truck
trees hanging heavy
branches bent so far

Cold winter night
crisp and clean
so white.

WORKING

Working, working
day and night
trying so hard
for naught
giving
without getting
laughing
at it all

It's so
hard to understand
why the money's
not enough.

YOU SURE FOOLED ME

You sure fooled me
Months and months
with you telling me
how much you've changed

I began to believe it

But then the opportunity arose
and your ugly self
came out again
shocking and reminding me
why I still must be a fool

A DAY ALONE

Waiting for a day
for herself

she planned
how she would spend it

alone for a minute
a second

without someone needing her
calling her

She has the day now
but she can't remember

who she was
and what she wanted then

AIR CONDITIONER

Summer days
so hot and humid
sweat pours off

Air conditioner
you are my savior

AUTUMN HAS BEGUN

Autumn has begun.
Welcome—
evenings are earlier,
darkness is still,
the wind brings the cold
refreshing my spirit
after the summer
heated my soul.

BASKETBALL

Basketball sitting
half buried in the snow
dreams of warm days
bouncing
flying into the hoop

BEAUTY STUNS ME

Beauty stuns me
halts my mind
Then I remember
the ugly

BUS RIDE

Waiting for
the bus
she smiles
not having
to worry
about the car

Mr. Bus Driver
will be in command

Settling in her seat
she opens her book
and enters another world

CHRISTMAS CACTUS

Pink flowers are blooming
on the plant
you gave me last year.

CLEANING

You clean and wipe
frantically, fantastically,
and yet you cannot clean
the dirt inside
that slips out
in your speech,
your driving,
nasty comments,
worries over germs,
not knowing you are
driving us mad.

CLICK

Come see me in my despair
It will not last too long
My moods change
like a traffic light
Click, click, click

COLOR BALANCE

Taking away
the light you have
your darkness shrouds
us all
but light is part
of darkness
so the spark
will come back brighter
as this deeper color fades

DAFFODILS

Do you know
the daffodils
smiling at you
sunny bright reminder
of our friendship?

DRUM CLASS

Carrying the drums
we walked
laughing
sun in our faces
wind blowing

Aren't you girls going to drum?
No, we have to go.
How could we,
not knowing how to?

HERE ARE

Here are a dress
mixed up with memories,
leather shoes
sewn with stitches
of pain,
scarf knotted too tightly
covered with a shawl of grief.

I THOUGHT

At the basilica
I thought I
saw you but death

took you last year
Now you work
security with the angels

LAMB STEW

The phone rang.
Some lamb stew for you
taking me back
years,
watching her cook
in her housedress,
mixing love into the stew.

LIKE A WARM FIRE

We're laughing and crying
together
riding the waves
of emotions
sorrows mixed
with joys
friendship like a warm fire.

LITTLE DOGS

Little dogs
sleeping soundly
dream of running
while I sit
and ponder
how they
see with
their eyes
closed

HEY, LITTLE ONE

Hey, little one, be careful
The four-way stop is not for you
little grey squirrel
with a mouthful

You aren't able yet to cross
Your tail is still to small

MOON MADNESS

The silvery full moon
caresses my eyes
ignites my soul
with memories
of wild fun nights
all blames on you

NOTHING AGAIN

Words are floating
onto this page
from the aether,
memories mixed
with newness,
changing the future:

I remember
searching frantically
before I found
nothing again.

POISONED

Poisoned love
from you
tainted by your pain
could not dim
the futile light
leading us to separation

REMINDERS

Plastic sunflowers
white and yellow
sat in a green vase

happy reminders
of your open arms.

SKUNK

The skunk
that slowly crossed the street
glanced at me
as I ran into the house

KERCHIEF

The navy blue kerchief
lies in the hall
Shall I pass it on
or keep it,
remembering how
it protected you
from the cold?

It is tattered
and has a hole in it,
but it is
with more than
gold to me,
an inheritance
in cloth,
like the scapular
you once wore.

TOGETHER

I've been waiting all day
for a poem to float in,
words laughing together at me.

TURKEY SOUP

Cold autumn evening
dark too early,
steaming turkey soup
complete with sweet corn
in a Campbell's soup cup
while we laugh in the kitchen
without the kids,
without the husband,
just friends again,
two women savoring
the night.

WEARING
MY SUNGLASSES

Wearing my sunglasses
on a cloudy day
filters the light
from your eyes
and keep my soul
from stretching out across the room

WELCOME

As the cold north wind
blew in last night
I welcomed it,
memories of winter warmth
near the fireplace,
under the covers,
and laughter in the snow.

WHO WOULD KNOW

Listening and absorbing
I wonder how it is
you feel nothing

while I feel the little sparrows'
wings, the sun blazing,
the dogs whimpering
while they sleep,
and the screaming of our soul
that you cannot hear.

INDEX OF TITLES

www.ingramcontent.com/pod-product-compliance
Lightning Source LLC
Chambersburg PA
CBHW032147040426

42449CB00005B/432